In the Forest

by Cynthia Swain

I need to know these words.

forest

grass

red fox

trees

What is a **forest**?

A forest is a home for plants.

A forest is a home for animals.

You can see many **trees** in a forest.

Some trees are big.

Some trees are little.

You can see flowers in a forest.
You can see **grass**, too.

9

Many animals live in the forest.
Some animals are birds.
This bird is a woodpecker.

This bird is a hawk.

This animal lives in the forest, too.
This animal is a porcupine.
The porcupine eats leaves.

This **red fox** lives in the forest.
The red fox eats little animals.

You can see ants in the forest.

You can see a frog, too.

Can you see this animal in the forest?